Never
Use White Type
on a Black
Background
And 50 other
Ridiculous Design Rules

COLOPHON

BIS Publishers
Het Sieraad
Postjesweg 1
1057 DT Amsterdam
The Netherlands
T (+) 31 (0)20-515 02 30
F (+) 31 (0)20 515 02 39
bis@bispublishers.nl
www.bispublishers.nl

ISBN 978-90-6369-207-0

Ridiculous Design Rules is a concept for Four Weeks
of FreeDesigndom (www.freedesigndom.com),
developed by Lemon Scented Tea and commissioned
by Premsela, Dutch Platform for Design and Fashion
(www.premsela.org).

Editorial Director: Anneloes van Gaalen
(www.paperdollwriting.com)
Designed by: Lilian van Dongen Torman
(www.born84.nl)

BIS PUBLISHERS

Never
Use White Type
on a Black
Background

And 50 other
Ridiculous Design Rules

CONTENTS

INTRODUCTION

The world of fashion and design is inundated with a seemingly endless list of rules. Think of 'less is more', 'form follows function', 'dress your age', 'keep it simple', and the list goes on and on. They're familiar sayings that some designers consider to be valuable words of wisdom, which serve as a guiding line and source of inspiration. To others, these rules are mere restrictions: design dogmas and fashion formulae that need to be bended, twisted or broken altogether.

Rules tend to have a life of their own: over time their meaning changes or the rule is adopted by a whole new group of followers. Take, for instance, the classic 'form follows function'. It started out life as an architecture guideline but has crept its way into other creative fields. This evolution is reflected in this book by the chronologically placed quotes that accompany each rule and that are courtesy of designers, architects, fashion designers, typographers and other creatives. All rules are also accompanied by an image that either negates or supports the rule. Our aim is not to list all the rules that you need to adhere to. Nor do we take sides in the whole rules debate. Granted, creativity knows no bounds and therefore it seems rather ridiculous to restrict that creativity by sticking to a couple of age-old rules. However, in some cases the rules seems more like the basic principles that every designer should love, honor and obey.

Whichever side of the fence you yourself are sitting on in the rules debate, you're bound to find this book a source of inspiration, comfort, joy or just good old fun. Enjoy.

PS For future publications on rules governing the world of typography, graphic design, web design, fashion and architecture we're looking for rules and your comments on them. Send the rules you love or hate to rules@bispublishers.nl.

Good designers copy, great designers steal

This rule is generally considered to be taken from Pablo Picasso's famous remark: "Good artists copy, great artists steal." But in a case of life imitating art, Picasso allegedly took the saying from Igor Stravinsky who in turn is thought to have taken it from T.S. Eliot.

———

"All the old fellows stole our best ideas."
Frederic W. Goudy (1865–1947), American type designer

"The secret to creativity is knowing how to hide your sources."
Albert Einstein (1879-1955), German-born American physicist

"Good composers don't borrow, they steal."
Igor Stravinsky (1882-1971), Russian-born American composer

"Immature poets imitate; mature poets steal; bad poets deface what they take, and good poets make it into something better, or at least something different."
T. S. Eliot (1888-1965), American-English poet, dramatist and literary critic

"It's not where you take things from – it's where you take them to."
Jean-Luc Godard (1930), Franco-Swiss filmmaker

"Don't bother concealing your thievery – celebrate it if you feel like it."
Jim Jarmusch (1953), American filmmaker

"Copycats beware: stay away from Marcel Wanders designs!"
Marcel Wanders (1963), Dutch designer, after winning yet another copyright lawsuit

"It's a very fine line of what is a copy and what is inspiration."
Zac Posen (1980), American fashion designer

Make it pretty

Many a designer has heard the words 'make it pretty' uttered by their client or sales rep. As annoying and frustrating as this little sentence might be to the creative, it does point to the importance of aesthetics in design. In the end, French-born American industrial designer Raymond Loewy (1893-1986) said it best: "Ugliness does not sell."

———

"Don't make something unless it is both necessary and useful; but if it is both necessary and useful, don't hesitate to make it beautiful."
Shaker philosophy

"When I am working on a problem I never think about beauty. I only think about how to solve the problem. But when I have finished, if the solution is not beautiful, I know it is wrong."
Buckminster Fuller (1895-1983), American architect, author and designer

"Design is not making beauty, beauty emerges from selection, affinities, integration, love."
Louis Kahn (1901-1974), American architect

"Without aesthetic, design is either the humdrum repetition of familiar clichés or a wild scramble for novelty. Without the aesthetic, the computer is but a mindless speed machine, producing effects without substance. Form without relevant content, or content without meaningful form."
Paul Rand (1914-1996), American graphic designer

"The life of a designer is a life of fight. A fight against ugliness, just like a doctor fights against disease. For us, visual disease is what we have all around. And what we try to do is to cure it somehow with design."
Massimo Vignelli (1931), Italian designer

"I have combined the ideas of beauty and function into one word: Beautility."
Tucker Viemeister (1948), American industrial designer

"Make it like a sunflower."
Steve Jobs (1955), co-founder of Apple and Pixar

"Ugliness can make you think – if you go too beautiful it can stop you from thinking."
Bertjan Pot (1975), Dutch designer

"Fashion is made to become unfashionable."

rule 03

1896

French fashion designer Coco Chanel (1883-1971) not only brought the world the little black dress, she also summed up the transitory nature of fashion in one heck of a one-liner.

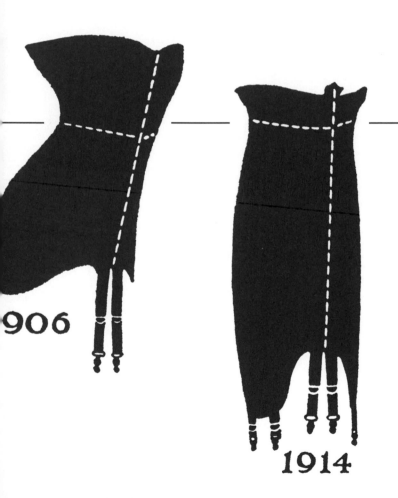

906

1914

"So soon as a fashion is universal, it is out of date."
Marie Von Ebner-Eschenbach (1830-1916), Austrian author

"Fashion is a form of ugliness so intolerable that we have to alter it every six months."
Oscar Wilde (1854-1900), Irish poet, playwright and author

"Fashion fades, only style remains the same."
Coco Chanel (1883-1971), French fashion designer

"Art produces ugly things, which frequently become more beautiful with time. Fashion, on the other hand, produces beautiful things, which always become ugly with time."
Jean Cocteau (1889-1963), French poet, artist and filmmaker

"Only the minute and the future are interesting in fashion – it exists to be destroyed."
Karl Lagerfeld (1938), German fashion designer

"I would never talk about style because style is part of cultural domains, that are part of fashion, and fashion is part of the idea of getting unfashionable, and getting unfashionable is part of consumerism. So every style is dangerous as far as its features are concerned: a new style substitutes an old one and people just change their habits just for media matters and not because a certain style could be more functional than another one."
Philippe Starck (1949), French product designer

"Fashion is an expression and a reaction. It's a reflection, and even a proposal, on the current situation of our society."
Helmut Lang (1956), Austrian fashion designer

"Fashion will be in fashion for a long time."
Angelique Westerhof (1969), director of the Dutch Fashion Foundation

1917

"It's all a game, with new rules every season."

Stefano Gabbana (1962),
Italian fashion designer

"Design is thinking made visual."

Even if you don't know the quote or the man quoted, you will definitely know the man's work. The title sequences that American graphic designer and filmmaker Saul Bass (1920-1996) designed have lit up the silver screen. His designs for film posters have become part of popular culture. And his 'design is thinking made visual' comment has become something of a design mantra.

———————

"Typographical design should perform optically what the speaker creates through voice and gesture of his thoughts."
El Lizzitsky (1890-1941), Russian artist and designer

"Typography at its best is a visual form of language linking timelessness and time."
Robert Bringhurst (1946), American poet, typographer and author

"I'm very much a word person, so that's why typography for me is the obvious extension. It just makes my words visible."
Erik Spiekermann (1947), German typographer and designer

rule
05

A camel is a horse designed by a committee

This rule, which implies that design by committee doesn't work, comes courtesy of Sir Alec Issigonis (1906-1988), the Greek-British car designer, best known for giving the world the Mini.

———

"It's really hard to design products by focus groups. A lot of times, people don't know what they want until you show it to them."
Steve Jobs (1955), co-founder of Apple and Pixar

"Fire the committee. No great website in history has been conceived of by more than three people. Not one. This is a deal breaker."
Seth Godin (1960), American author

"It is an old joke that a camel is a horse designed by a committee, a joke which does grave injustice to a splendid creature and altogether too much honor to the creative power of committees."
Michael French, American author of Invention and Evolution: Design in Nature and Engineering *(1994)*

rule
06

NEVER USE MORE THAN TWO TYPEFACES

The unwritten rule of typography is that a document should never feature more than two typeface families, although some draw the line at three. Anything to avoid a cluttered look.

"There are now about as many different varieties of letters as there are different kinds of fools."
Eric Gill (1882-1940), British sculptor and typeface designer

"Type production has gone mad, with its senseless outpouring of new types… only in degenerate times can personality (opposed to the nameless masses) become the aim of human development."
Jan Tschichold (1902-1974), German typographer, book designer and writer

"Use two typeface families maximum. OK, maybe three."
Timothy Samara, American designer and educator

"A designer should only use these 5 typefaces: Bodoni, Helvetica, Times Roman, Century, Futura."
Massimo Vignelli (1931), Italian designer

"A single type family with a variety of weights and italics should be enough all by itself; adding a second is nice for texture, but don't overdo it. Too many typefaces are distracting and self-conscious and might confuse or tire the reader."
Timothy Samara, American designer and educator

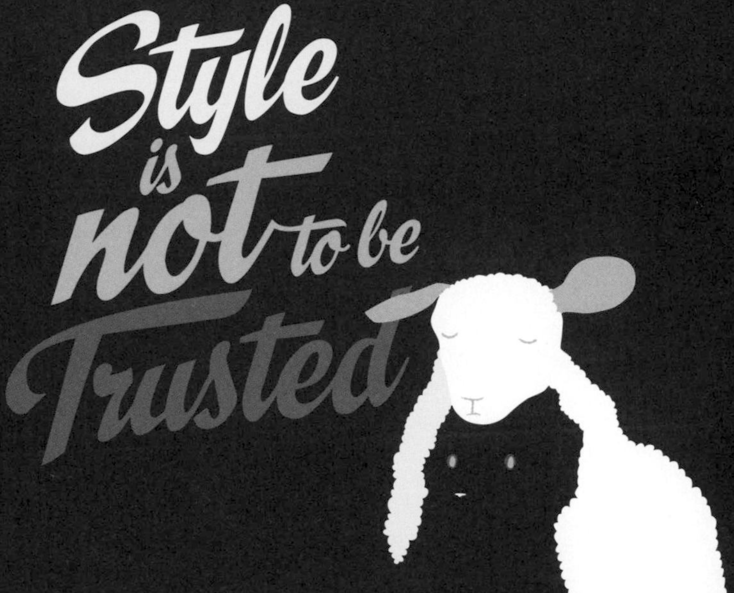
Style
is
not to be
Trusted

Style. It's a certain *je ne sais quoi*. It's elusive, hard to define, and according to graphic designer Milton Glaser, it's something that should not be trusted. In 2001 the man who brought the world the I Love New York logo gave a talk in which he discussed the ten things he had learned in his impressive career. Lesson number seven on the list? Style is not to be trusted.

"Style is when they're running you out of town and you make it look like you're leading the parade."
William Battie (1703-1776), English physician

"Style for the sake of style alone will have less meaning to the consumer than value. An interruption of the spiral created by boosting sales from year to year with false inducements of style, bulk and flash gives design a new lease on life. Aesthetic beauty will be the direct result of careful planning and precision manufacturing."
Raymond Loewy (1893-1986), French-born American industrial designer

"Style is primarily a matter of instinct."

Bill Blass (1922-2002), American fashion designer

"Style is knowing who you are, what you want to say and not giving a damn."
Gore Vidal (1925), American novelist, playwright and essayist

"The essence of style is a simple way of saying something complex."
Giorgio Armani (1934), Italian fashion designer

"Style is not something to be pursued on its own but as a result of other factors."
Chuck Hoberman (1956), American designer

"Design is steeped in style; I would say 90 per cent of it is style. And style is not a bad word, but the design community wants to believe it's a bad word. Well, it's about time they started to admit that part of our position and our premise is to shift people's sensibilities. And you shift sensibilities and you make movements through style. In painting, we speak about style. In fashion, we speak about style. But for some reason in design we don't want to speak about this thing called style because there's something superficial about it."
Karim Rashid (1960), British-Egyptian industrial designer

"Style = Fart."
Stefan Sagmeister (1962), Austrian
*graphic designer**

"Style is an invention of the insecure."
Marcel Wanders (1963), Dutch
designer

* "Yes, I said this but I had to give up.
It was the headline of a theory that style
and stylistic questions are just hot air
and meaningless. I discovered that this
is simply not true. Through experience
I found that if you have content that is
worthwhile the proper expression of
that content, in terms of form and style,
is actually very important. It can be a
very useful tool to communicate that
content. I don't think that it is actually
hot air anymore."
Stefan Sagmeister (1962), Austrian
graphic designer

Good design solves the right problem

In his 2002 essay *Taste for Makers*, programmer turned author Paul Graham (1964) listed what he considered the Principles of Design. According to Graham, who founded the first ASP (application service provider), good design is simple, hard, timeless, suggestive, often slightly funny, looks easy, uses symmetry, resembles nature and solves the right problem.

———

"Design is a problem-solving activity."
Paul Rand (1914-1996), American graphic designer

"Of course design is about problem solving, but I cannot resist adding something personal."
Wim Crouwel (1928), Dutch graphic designer and typographer

"Design is directed toward human beings. To design is to solve human problems by identifying them, examining alternate solutions to them, choosing and executing the best solution."
Ivan Chermayeff (1932), British graphic designer

"I think that the world today is in crying need of design and designers who can think about solving the seemingly overwhelming problems that we have. If you look at the incredible upheaval we have going on concerning climate change and other crises around the world that can in part be addressed by design. In that sense I think that it's a very inspirational time."
Chuck Hoberman (1956), American designer

"As designers, we always see an opportunity to solve problems."
Tahmineh Javanbakht (1961), Iranian designer

"The thing that has always driven me as a designer is feeling pissed off by the shitty stuff around me and wanting to make it better."
Marc Newson (1963), Australian designer

"I don't solve problems, I create possibilities."
Richard Hutten (1967), Dutch designer

"I'm not a designer trying to solve problems."
Ron Gilad (1972), Israeli industrial designer

Design isn't art

Usability is often considered to be the decisive factor in the whole art versus design debate. The general consensus seems to be: if you can't use it, it's probably art. But with the dividing line between art and design growing increasingly blurry, the debate continues.

"Design is the method of putting form and content together. Design, just as art, has multiple definitions; there is no single definition. Design can be art. Design can be aesthetics. Design is so simple, that's why it is so complicated."
Paul Rand (1914-1996), American graphic designer

"If one of the definitions we have concerning art is that it serves its public by reflecting and explaining the world at a particular moment in history, it is hard to believe that design does not serve in a similar way."
Milton Glaser (1929), American graphic designer and illustrator

"It doesn't matter one damn bit whether fashion is art or not. You don't question whether an incredible chef is an artist or not – his cakes are delicious and that's all that matters."
Sonia Rykiel (1930), French fashion designer

"Art has to move you and design does not, unless it's a good design for a bus."
David Hockney (1937), British artist

"Art and fashion are one and the same to me, intrinsically linked."
Wolfgang Joop (1944), German fashion designer

"Design should do the same thing in everyday life that art does when encountered: amaze us, scare us or delight us, but certainly open us to new worlds within our daily existence."
Aaron Betsky (1958), American architect, curator and writer on architecture and design

"Designers always flirt with art."

Hella Jongerius (1963), Dutch designer

"As a fashion designer, I was always aware that I was not an artist, because I was creating something that was made to be sold, marketed, used, and ultimately discarded. True artists – and I do think there are some fashion-designer artists – create because they can't do anything but create. There is no purpose to their work other than expression."
Tom Ford (1961), American fashion designer

"Design is one of the arts, so designers are artists. But if designers make objects which can't be used, then they are not making design, and this should not be considered as design. Maybe it's decoration, maybe it's art, but definitely not design."
Richard Hutten (1967), Dutch designer

Minimalism is dead

In his study of minimalism Edward Strickland summed it up perfectly: "The death of Minimalism is announced periodically, which may be the surest testimonial to its staying power." Minimalism is dead, long live minimalism.

"Minimalism wasn't a real idea – it ended before it started."
Sol LeWitt (1928- 2007), American artist

"I think some people would love to be able to make the clothes I make – and of course, I do influence them, but they keep simplifying, and minimalism doesn't quite work."
Vivienne Westwood (1941), British fashion designer

"Minimalism without a sense of quality and class doesn't mean very much."
Jil Sander (1943), German fashion designer

"I don't like minimalism. The 'less is more' dogma of the fifties is simply not true. Less is not more. It is a notion of the elite, which looks down on everything that is kitsch and different. But I say: ultimately, minimalism is the ideal breeding ground for kitsch. Even in the case of someone who's been living in a perfect minimalist house for ten years, one can be sure that a large plastic lobster or a small antique painting from aunt so-and-so is carried into the house. There comes a time when you simply have to introduce something kitschy into your house. The conclusion: minimalism doesn't work."
Italo Rota (1953), Italian architect

Never use copy and paste

Ctrl+C. Ctrl+V. Thanks to these basic keyboard shortcuts, plagiarism is a mere click away.

"I am a great believer in copying; there has never been an age in which people have so little respect for the past."
Vivienne Westwood (1941), British fashion designer

"Use your fucking brain. People don't think enough. People don't use their brain. They use copy-paste. Your brain is free. It is fast. Wickedly fast."
Erik Spiekermann (1947), German typographer and designer

"How can we ever find an individual signature in this copy culture."
Geert Lovink (1959), Dutch media theorist

"We rip, steal, burn, cut and paste. Reproduction is the essence of successful design."
Hendrik-Jan Grievink (1977), Dutch editorial designer

Never use copy and paste

rule
11

Ctrl+C. Ctrl+V. Thanks to these basic keyboard shortcuts, plagiarism is a mere click away.

"I am a great believer in copying; there has never been an age in which people have so little respect for the past."
Vivienne Westwood (1941), British fashion designer

"Use your fucking brain. People don't think enough. People don't use their brain. They use copy-paste. Your brain is free. It is fast. Wickedly fast."
Erik Spiekermann (1947), German typographer and designer

"How can we ever find an individual signature in this copy culture."
Geert Lovink (1959), Dutch media theorist

"We rip, steal, burn, cut and paste. Reproduction is the essence of successful design."
Hendrik-Jan Grievink (1977), Dutch editorial designer

Make it new

"Make it new!" This call to arms by American poet Ezra Pound (1885-1972) became the battle cry of the Modernist movement.

"Make it new is the message not just of Modern art but of Modern consumerism, of which Modern art is largely a mirror image."
Christopher Lasch (1932-1994), American historian

"The best designed product is the one that hasn't been invented yet."
Ingegerd Råman (1943), Swedish product and glassware designer

"To design is to do things that did not exist before I designed them. I'm not interested in styling or variations on something that existed before. Newness can come from all sorts of places. There isn't one source of newness – it could be in the function, form, material, process, weight, size, smell or whatever – just to have enough of it to justify the existence of a new piece in a world that is over-populated with objects anyway."
Ron Arad (1951), Israeli architect and industrial designer

Never photograph people eating

Nobody really seems to know who came up with this one, but take one look at the undoubtedly unflattering photos taken of you or your loved ones while munching away on some food and this rule's *raison d'être* will immediately become apparent.

The photos are taken from Hans Eijkelboom's
Paris - New York - Shanghai project

"There are no rules for good photographs, there are only good photographs."

Ansel Adams (1902-1984), American photographer

"I really believe there are things nobody would see if I didn't photograph them."
Diane Arbus (1923-1971), American photographer

"My photographs do me an injustice. They look just like me."
Phyllis Diller (1917), American comedienne

"Photography is not a sport. It has no rules. Everything must be dared and tried!"
Bill Brandt (1904-1983), British photographer and photojournalist

ALWAYS MAKE THE TOP LEFT-HAND LOGO OF THE WEBSITE A HOME BUTTON

Most people do not react well to change, those surfing the net are no exception. In fact, if Jakob Nielsen's research has taught us anything about web usability, it is that you want to be as predictable as possible: "Consistency is one of the most powerful usability principles: when things always behave the same, users don't have to worry about what will happen. Instead, they know what will happen based on earlier experience. Every time you release an apple over Sir Isaac Newton, it will drop on his head. That's good."

Be consistent: always make the top left-hand logo of the website a home button.

"Ever since Google has become a verb, people have been using websites differently. Home pages aren't important any more. You search for what you are searching for and you will appear somewhere.

The home page is now almost like the cover of a book. It's there, but it's not what you read. It's becoming much, much more important to design deep, deep web pages. It's important that you can find a complete hierarchy and that you know where you are.

In old-fashioned websites, you would have a home page and if you went deep you could never get back – you never knew where you were, but that wouldn't matter, you went down then you went out.

Now, no matter where you are, you can go in any direction. It means that clutter will make it worse and sites will have to be designed a little more tidily."
Erik Spiekermann (1947), German typographer and designer

Keep It Simple, Stupid

The K.I.S.S. principle aka 'Keep It Simple, Stupid' aka 'Keep It Small and Scalable' aka 'Keep It Short and Simple' aka 'Keep It Sweet and Simple' means a lot of different things to a lot of different people, depending on the industry they work in.

The rule is generally believed to be a variation of Occam's or Ockham's Razor. William of Ockham, a fourteenth-century Franciscan philosopher, argued that *Pluralitas non est ponenda sine necessitate* ('Plurality should not be posited without necessity'), meaning that the simplest explanation of a theory is always preferable. When it comes to design simplicity is also key, or so the rule goes.

———

"Simplicity is the ultimate sophistication."
Leonardo da Vinci (1452 - 1519), Italian artist, engineer and scientist

"The main goal is not to complicate the already difficult life of the consumer"
Raymond Loewy (1893-1986), French-born American industrial designer

"Think simple as my old master used to say – meaning, reduce the whole of its parts into the simplest terms, getting back to first principles."
Frank Lloyd Wright (1867-1959), American architect

"Make it simple. Make it memorable. Make it inviting to look at. Make it fun to read."
Leo Burnett (1891-1971), American advertising executive

"Simplicity is not the goal. It is the by-product of a good idea and modest expectations."
Paul Rand (1914-1996), American graphic designer

"Simplicity means the total absence, not so much of decoration, as of decoration superimposed, redundant and serving no purpose."
Vico Magistretti (1920-2006), Italian industrial designer

"Anyone can make the simple complicated. Creativity is making the complicated simple."
Charles Mingus (1922-1979), American jazz composer and bassist

"Simplify, and add lightness."
Colin Chapman (1928-1982), British designer and founder of Lotus Cars

"Make the simple things simple, and the complex things possible."
Xavier Lust (1969), Belgian designer

Don't over accessorize

American actress and queen of the one-liners Mae West (1893-1980) once said: "Too much of a good thing can be wonderful." Great line, great lady. Still, accessory overload is considered a serious fashion *faux pas*. Best take Coco Chanel's (1883-1971) advice and "take one thing off before you leave the house."

"Know, first, who you are, and then adorn yourself accordingly."
Epictetus (AD. 55-AD. 135), Greek philosopher

"No elegance is possible without perfume. It is the unseen, unforgettable, ultimate accessory of fashion that heralds your arrival and prolongs your departure."
Coco Chanel (1883-1971), French fashion designer

"Accessories are important and becoming more and more important every day."
Giorgio Armani (1934), Italian fashion designer

USE A GRID

The grid: a staple in the toolbox of designers and graphic artists alike, providing the framework and underlying structure for their designs.

———

"The grid system is an aid, not a guarantee. It permits a number of possible uses and each designer can look for a solution appropriate to his personal style. But one must learn how to use the grid; it is an art that requires practice."
Josef Müller-Brockmann (1914-1996), Swiss graphic designer

"GRIDS ARE VERY HANDY BUT SHOULD NEVER BE AN END IN ITSELF."

Robin Uleman (1969), Dutch graphic designer

"A design should have some tension and some expression in itself. I like to compare it with the lines on a football field. It is a strict grid. In this grid you play a game and these can be nice games or very boring games..."
Wim 'Gridnik' Crouwel (1928), Dutch graphic designer and typographer

"Grids do not exist in a vacuum. They exist in relation to the content. We never start with a grid. We start with an idea which is then translated into a form, a structure."
Linda van Deursen (1961), Dutch graphic designer and one half of Mevis & Van Deursen

"To say a grid is limiting is to say that language is limiting, or typography is limiting. It is up to us to use these media critically or passively."
Ellen Lupton (1963), American graphic designer, writer and curator

"We use grids in our work, but we think we use them in a completely different way than, for example, Swiss Late-Modernist designers such as Josef Müller-Brockmann. Although we really admire grid-driven work, we wouldn't dare to call ourselves proper Gridniks."
Experimental Jetset (founded in 1997), Dutch graphic design unit

A PICTURE IS THOUSAND

Back in 1921 the advertising trade journal *Printers' Ink* ran an ad which read: "One Look is Worth A Thousand Words". In the advertisement Fred R. Barnard talked about the benefits of advertising on street cars. According to Barnard, the ad's headline was taken from a 'famous Japanese philosopher'. Six years later Barnard would use the sentence in another ad, this time slightly changing it into: "One Picture is Worth Ten Thousand Words." A cliché was born.

"An image is not simply a trademark, a design, a slogan or an easily remembered picture. It is a studiously crafted personality profile of an individual, institution, corporation, product or service."
Daniel J. Boorstin (1914-2004), American historian

"As the Chinese say, 1001 words is worth more than a picture."
John McCarthy (1927), American computer scientist

WORTH A WORDS

"A picture says more than a thousand words, only as much as a thousand words say more than a picture. A thousand apples don't taste any better than a pear, and a thousand pears don't taste any better than an apple. The apple tastes different to the pear, no matter how many of them there are. A thousand words say something different to a picture"
Bo Bergström (1946), Swedish author, lecturer and creative director

"A picture is worth a thousand dollars."
Marty Neumeier (1947), American communication designer, writer and publisher

"A picture is worth a thousand words. An interface is worth a thousand pictures."
Ben Shneiderman (1947), American computer scientist

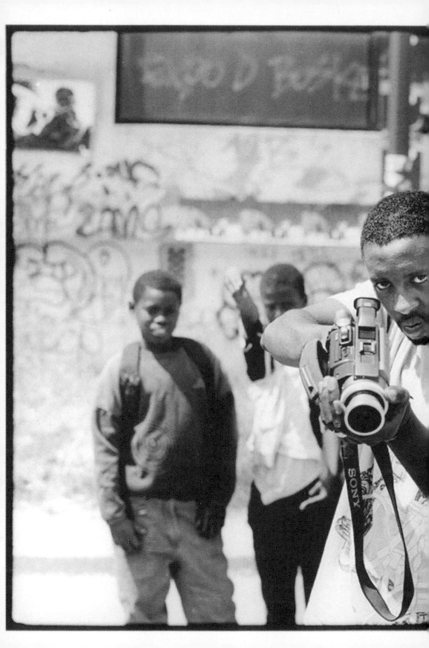

Never stretc
a font..........

Never stretch a font

In the world of typography legibility and readability reign supreme. And rightly so. After all, you want people to be able to see and read the words in front of them. Speaking of reading, the third volume of *Indie Fonts* notes that there is nothing wrong with "compressing (or stretching) a font within its capacity." But stretch it any further and you're in trouble: "The problem arises when a font has been compressed [or stretched] beyond its ability to retain a pleasing and readable effect." You have been warned.

"A lot of screen companies only make their fonts look good for one particular size but then they totally change their character when they get bigger or smaller."
Erik Spiekermann (1947), German typographer and designer

"When it comes to type and type usage, never stretch a font beyond its boundaries. Don't modify something to the point where it looks distorted. When that happens the reader doesn't notice the message before he notices the oddity. You don't want the type to catch the attention of the reader's eye more than the message."
Dennis Ortiz-Lopez, American typography designer

Practice makes perfect

This well-known proverb dates back to the mid-16th century, but still rings true today.

"It seems that perfection is reached not when there is nothing left to add, but when there is nothing left to take away."
Antoine de Saint-Exupery (1900-1944), French writer

"Ever tried. Ever failed. No matter. Try again. Fail again. Fail better."
Samuel Beckett (1906-1989), Irish playwright, poet and writer

"Perfectionism is the enemy of creation."
John Updike (1932), American novelist

"Perfection is not human. Perfection is for God, eventually, if he or she exists. Perfection is not our task. We have to express ourselves in our capacity, and our capacity is full of mistakes and incapacities. Let's express that. And transform that into the future beauty."
Gaetano Pesce (1939), Italian designer and architect

"We're never 100 percent satisfied with the end collection... We always find something that isn't perfect. We say all the time: 'next season'."
Stefano Gabbana (1962), Italian fashion designer

Form follows function

In 1896 American architect Louis Sullivan (1856-1924), often hailed as the 'father of Modernism', published an article titled *The Tall Office Building Artistically Considered*. In the article Sullivan wrote "form ever follows function," which was shortened to the well-known dictum 'form follows function'. But while the phrase gained worldwide recognition because of Sullivan, it was actually American sculptor Horatio Greenough (1805-1852) who first coined the term. In turn the Neo-Classicist Greenough most likely got the idea from the 18th century Italian Jesuit monk Carlo Lodoli and his theories on architecture and the role function plays in it.

"It would seem that more than function itself, simplicity is the deciding factor in the aesthetic equation. One might call the process beauty through function and simplification."
Raymond Loewy (1893-1986), French-born American industrial designer

"Form follows function – that has been misunderstood. Form and function should be one, joined in a spiritual union."
Frank Lloyd Wright (1867-1959), American architect

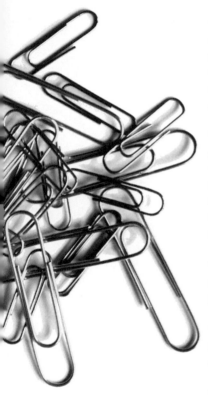

"With function, flow, and form as basis, design is evaluated as a process culminating in an entity which intensifies comprehension."
Ladislav Sutnar (1897-1976), Czech graphic designer

"Design is... above all an effort to improve reality... I always try to begin with considerations of its function... I ask myself, who needs it, which materials best suit its functions and so on..."
Gianfranco Frattini (1926), Italian industrial designer

"Form follows failure."
Henry Petroski (1942), American professor of civil engineering

"Form follows emotion."
Hartmut Esslinger (1944), German-American industrial designer

"The form and function of a successful design object should be mutually reinforcing; consequently, altering the form of an object will degrade the function and vice versa."
Tahmineh Javanbakht (1961), Iranian designer

THE LOGO MUST BE RECOGNIZABLE

It's the golden rule of logo design, best illustrated by advertising icons like McDonald's Golden Arches and Nike's Swoosh.

———————

"A logo is a flag, a signature, an escutcheon, a street sign.
A logo does not sell (directly), it *identifies*.
A logo is rarely a description of a business.
A logo derives *meaning* from the quality of the thing it symbolizes, not the other way around.
A logo is less important than the product it signifies; what it represents is more important than what it looks like."
Paul Rand (1914-1996), American graphic designer

"When a logo has been in the public domain for more than fifty years it becomes a classic, a landmark, a respectable entity and there is no reason to throw it away and substitute it with a new concoction, regardless of how well it has been designed."
Massimo Vignelli (1931), Italian designer

"A good logo is easily remembered; a good logo has an iconic nature, and becomes part of our life and memories; a good logo has cultural depth although it is simple; a good logo is surprising in its simplicity and freshness, even a hundred years after it was created; a good logo serves the people needs more than the client's or the designer's needs."
Oded Ezer (1972), Israeli typographer and graphic designer

If you

don't know what to do... just do it big and red

Few colors evoke stronger emotions and have a wider range of connotations than the color red. As for this specific rule, it is basically a variation of the old adage: "If you can't make it good, make it big. If you can't make it big, make it red." This saying has been attributed to a whole range of designers, but it remains somewhat of a mystery as to who first coined the phrase.

"Color does not add a pleasant quality to design – it reinforces it."
Pierre Bonnard (1867-1947), French artist

"When in doubt, wear red."
Bill Blass (1922-2002), American fashion designer

"If I don't know what to do, I use blue."
Wim Crouwel (1928), Dutch graphic designer and typographer

"Any color works if you push it to the extreme."
Massimo Vignelli (1931), Italian designer

"Women usually prefer to wear black at events, because it makes them feel safe. However, if there's one woman wearing red, she will inevitably be the eye-catcher of the evening. It's as though the room is suddenly illuminated, simply perfect for a grand entrance."
Valentino (1932), Italian fashion designer

"When in doubt, make it big. If still in doubt, make it red."
Michael Bierut (1957), American graphic designer and critic

"Red is one of the strongest colors, it's blood, it has a power with the eye. That's why traffic lights are red I guess, and stop signs as well... In fact I use red in all of my paintings."
Keith Haring (1958-1990), American artist

"An assistant in the office always used to wear the same color red lipstick and matching nail polish. One day I asked to borrow it and coated the bottom of a pair of stilettos just to see what it would look like, *et voilà*! I loved the dramatic red color against the clean line of the shoe. It was the most beautiful red I'd ever seen. Now it's my hallmark."
Christian Louboutin (1963), French shoe designer

"It is better to be good than to be original."

German-born American architect Mies van der Rohe (1886-1969), best known for his dictum 'less is more', also argued that "it is better to be good than to be original."

"I invent nothing. I rediscover."
Auguste Rodin (1840-1917), French artist

"Creativity often consists merely of turning up what is already there. Did you know that right and left shoes were thought up only a little more than a century ago?"
Bernice Fitz-Gibbon (1894-1982), American advertising executive

"Originality is merely an illusion."
M.C. Escher (1898-1972), Dutch graphic designer

"Originality is a product, not an intention."
Paul Rand (1914-1996), American graphic designer

"If you are not concerned with what 'good design' is and you let the design come from the idea, you get an original design."
Bob Gill (1931), American graphic designer

"Sometimes there is simply no need to be either clever or original."
Ivan Chermayeff (1932), British graphic designer

"I'm not trying to do something different, I'm trying to do the same thing but in a different way."
Vivienne Westwood (1941), British fashion designer

"To achieve originality we need to abandon the comforts of habit, reason, and the approval of our peers."
Marty Neumeier (1947), American communication designer, writer and publisher

"I give classics just a little kick."
Paul Smith (1947), British fashion designer

"Original thought is like original sin: both happened before you were born to people you could not have possibly met."
Fran Leibowitz (1950), American author

"Originality is non-existent."
Jim Jarmusch (1953), American filmmaker

EXIT / ÇIK

"Fashion can be bought. Style, one must possess."

Anna Wintour has become pretty much synonymous with *Vogue*. But before there was Anna, there was Edna. As editor-in-chief, Edna Woolman Chase (1877-1957) turned *Vogue* into the style bible it is today. In the process she also produced some great one-liners that have stood the test of time.

———

"Oh, never mind the fashion. When one has a style of one's own, it is always twenty times better."
Margaret Oliphant (1828-1897), Scottish writer

"Fashions fade, style is eternal."
Yves Saint Laurent (1936-2008), French fashion designer

"The difference between style and fashion is quality."
Giorgio Armani (1934), Italian fashion designer

"I've always been about style for people, not 'you're going to wear this outfit', ... It was the way you put yourself together and the imagination, not buying this number off the rack, but the way you wear it."
Ralph Lauren (1939), American fashion designer

Helvetica always works
Helvetica always works
Helvetica always works
Helvetica always works

There are two types of typographers in this world: those who love Helvetica and those who hate it. These days the clean-cut typeface, which was designed back in 1957, seems more popular than ever thanks to Lars Müller's book *Helvetica: Homage to a Typeface* and the feature-length documentary by Gary Hustwit that travelled the world over.

"You can say, 'I love you,' in Helvetica. And you can say it with Helvetica Extra Light if you want to be really fancy. Or you can say it with the Extra Bold if it's really intensive and passionate, you know, and it might work."
Massimo Vignelli (1931), Italian designer

HELVETICA

2
Avenue

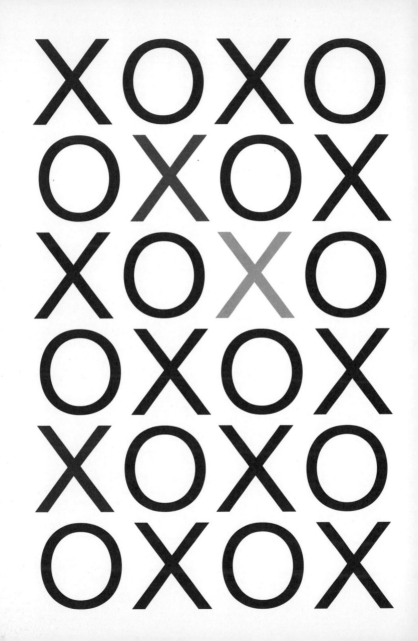

"Helvetica is like a good screwdriver; a reliable, efficient, easy-to-use tool. But put it in the wrong hands, and it's potentially lethal."

Tom Geismar (1931), American designer

"It's air, you know. It's just there. There's no choice. You have to breathe, so you have to use Helvetica."
Erik Spiekermann (1947), German typographer and designer

"I think I'm right calling Helvetica the perfume of the city. It is just something we don't notice usually but we would miss very much if it wouldn't be there."
Lars Müller (1955), Norwegian graphic designer and publisher

"[Helvetica] is all around us. You've probably already seen Helvetica several times today. It might have told you which subway platform you needed, or tried to sell you investment services or vacation getaways in the ads in your morning paper. Maybe it gave you the latest headlines on television, or let you know whether to 'push' or 'pull' to open your office door."
Gary Hustwit (1964), American film-maker and director of Helvetica

"Helvetica maybe says everything, and that's perhaps part of its appeal."
Jonathan Hoefler (1970), American font designer

"What we find interesting about Helvetica is its paradoxical nature: on the one hand, it is a neutral typeface, or better said, it is perceived as such. On the other hand, it carries this very heavy ideological baggage. There is this really interesting tension between its functionality and the meaning that it gained over the years. It is a typeface that is empty and loaded at the same time."
Experimental Jetset (founded in 1997), Dutch graphic design unit

CLEAVAGE OR LEGS, NEVER BOTH

'Either-or' or 'both-and'? The jury is still out on this one. Although, if you want to avoid overexposure, 'either-or' seems to be the way to go.

"Nothing goes out of fashion sooner than a long dress with a very low neck."
Coco Chanel (1883-1971), French fashion designer

"Your dresses should be tight enough to show you're a woman and loose enough to show you're a lady."
Edith Head (1897-1981), American costume designer

"Never in the history of fashion has so little material been raised so high to reveal so much that needs to be covered so badly."
Cecil Beaton (1904-1980), English fashion and portrait photographer

"The greatest concubines in history knew that everything revealed with nothing concealed is a bore."
Geoffrey Beene (1924-2004), American fashion designer

"There is a real vulgarity in the way women dress at the moment. They show off too much and try too hard. They don't understand where the line is between sexy and vulgar. I know where that line is."
Roberto Cavalli (1940), Italian fashion designer

"We have always been faithful to our roots and to our inspiration: we are Mediterranean, we love sensual ironic fashion and that always includes cleavage."
Domenico Dolce (1958) and Stefano Gabbana (1962), Italian fashion designers

* JULY 10-17 *

T W T F S   S M T W T F S   S M T W T F S   S M T W T F S   T W T F S
31 30 29 28 27   26 25 24 23 22 21 20   19 18 17 16 15 14 13   12 11 10 9 8 7 6   5 4 3 2 1

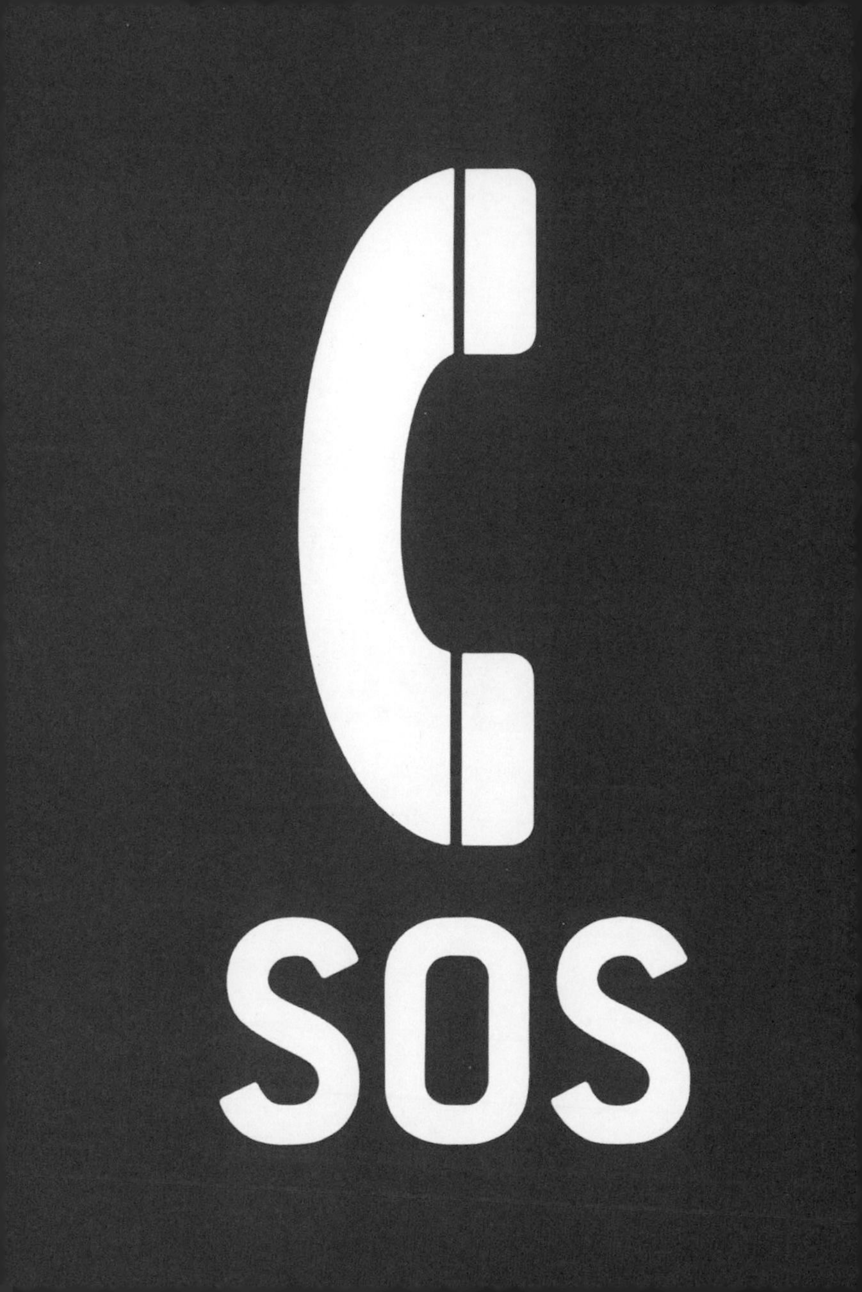
SOS

Good design communicates

Good design communicates… meaning
Good design communicates… effectively
Good design communicates… in a way that words simply can't
Good design communicates… and motivates; it does not merely decorate
Good design communicates… an idea and equally considers function and form
Good design communicates… the message you want to get across and inspires the best possible results
Good design communicates… a clear message to the desired audience, and serves the needs of the client, not the whims of the designer
Good design communicates… well*

*All taglines taken from different graphic design, web design and advertising agencies that promote their services by referring to this specific design rule.

"To design is to communicate clearly by whatever means you can control or master."
Milton Glaser (1929), American graphic designer and illustrator

"Good design, at least part of the time, includes the criteria of being direct in relation to the problem at hand – not obscure, trendy, or stylish. A new language, visual or verbal, must be couched in a language that is already understood."
Ivan Chermayeff (1932), British graphic designer

"Design must seduce, shape, and perhaps more importantly, evoke emotional response."
April Greiman (1948), American designer

"What's dangerous is when designers use a language that people can't understand."
Paula Scher (1948), American artist and graphic designer

"Don't confuse legibility with communication. Just because something is legible doesn't mean it communicates and, more importantly, doesn't mean it communicates the right thing."
David Carson (1952), American graphic designer

"People call me a showman, which I don't think is really the right word. I think it makes sense to use all our senses to communicate. I call myself a designer, and I design objects, but it doesn't mean I can only talk in the language of products."
Marcel Wanders (1963), Dutch designer

"The job of
the designer is
essentially to
communicate.
And the mediums
we are allowed to
communicate with
range from
drawing and other
forms of visual
expression to
building ideas
through research
and ethnographic
studies."

Yves Béhar (1967), Swiss-born industrial designer

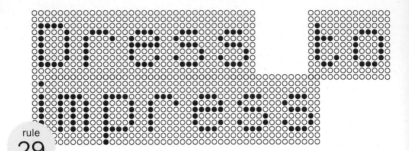

The term power dressing is forever linked to the 1980s – the time of big hair and even bigger shoulders – but the power of clothing is by no means limited to the era of Dynasty and Dallas. For centuries people from all corners of the world have used dress as an expression of their (preferred) identity, culture or social status.

"If people turn to look at you on the street, you are not well dressed."
George Bryan 'Beau' Brummel (1778-1840), British dandy

"Clothes make the man. Naked people have little or no influence on society."
Mark Twain (1835-1910), American author

"The only way to atone for being occasionally a little overdressed is by being always absolutely overeducated."
Oscar Wilde (1854-1900), Irish poet, playwright and author

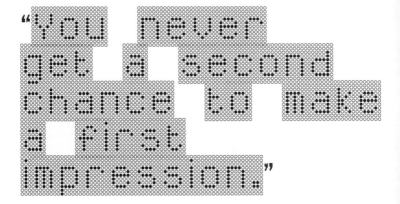

"You never get a second chance to make a first impression."

Will Rogers (1879-1935), American

"Dress shabbily, they notice the dress. Dress impeccably, they notice the woman."
Coco Chanel (1883-1971), French fashion designer

"It's always better to be looked over than over-looked."
Mae West (1893-1980), American actress

"You can have whatever you want if you dress for it."
Edith Head (1897-1981), American costume designer

"You have a much better life if you wear impressive clothes."
Vivienne Westwood (1941), British fashion designer

"Women and men should always interpret clothes according to their style, be ironic and self-confident and let clothes take a supporting role to their personality. A dress should never look like it's overpowering the wearer."
Domenico Dolce (1958) and Stefano Gabbana (1962), Italian fashion designers

"Dressing up. People just don't do it anymore. We have to change that."
John Galliano (1960), British fashion designer

"Never work with animals or children."

These famous words, once uttered by American actor and comedian W.C. Fields (1880-1946), have resonated with actors, artists and photographers the world over.

___

"I enjoy working with children because they are genuine; they don't wear masks."
Loretta Lux (1969), German artist

"Don't believe it when they say you should never work with children. Let's just say that everyone here tonight is easier to work with than Naomi. They turn up on time, they don't complain and they don't charge thousands for it."
Julien MacDonald (1972), British fashion designer, at his Barbie clothing catwalk show

"I love working with children, however you do need to have patience, because it can take some time to get what you are after, and sometimes it just doesn't work. It usually works when I'm photographing a child who has an intuitive understanding of what I'm trying to achieve. As for animals... that is hard work! They are tricky to direct."
Petrina Hicks (1972), Australian photographer

"Never use white type on a black background."

Words of wisdom by David Ogilvy, also known as the Godfather of modern advertising. In his book *Ogilvy on Advertising*, which by the way is mandatory reading for anyone in the creative industry, the English-born advertising exec hammers on the fact that white type on a black background simply doesn't work.

BLACK
ACKGROUND

"I am sometimes attacked for imposing 'rules'. Nothing could be further from the truth. I *hate* rules. All I do is report on how consumers react to different stimuli. I may say to a copywriter, 'Research shows that commercials with celebrities are below average in persuading people to buy products. Are you *sure* you want to use a celebrity?' Call that a *rule*? Or I may say to an art director, 'Research suggests that if you set the copy in black type on a white background, more people will read it than if you set it in white type on a black background.' A *hint*, perhaps, but scarcely a rule."
David Ogilvy (1911-1999), English-born advertising executive

"In printing, dropping white type out of a dark background was once a technically precarious practice. There was the danger that the thin parts of the letters would fill in. Moreover, the difficulty of reading white against black, with the vibrations that occur on the page, often proscribe printing this way."
Steven Guarnaccia and Susan Hochbaum, designers and authors of Black & White *(2002)*

Make the logo bigger

In the world of advertising sex sells and size matters. Or so the cliché goes. In his book *Hey, Whipple, Squeeze This: A Guide to Creating Great Ads, Second Edition* Luke Sullivan sums it up perfectly: "Clients are about their logos like guys are about their … you know. They love talking about them. They love to look at them. They want you to look at them. They think the bigger they are, the more effective they are. And they try to sneak looks at other guys' logos when they can. But as any woman will tell you, nobody cares." Indeed, it's not the size of the logo that matters, it's what you do with it.

"Most corporations think the logo is a kind of rabbit's foot or talisman – although sometimes it can be an albatross – and believe that if it is altered, something terrible will happen."
Paul Rand (1914-1996), American graphic designer

"Logos are dead. Long live icons and avatars."
Marty Neumeier (1947), American communication designer, writer and publisher

"I was once asked by a client to create a logo that would win an Addy Award. Luckily, I have a drawerful of pencils for just such an occasion."

Rodney Davidson (1957), American graphic designer

"A logo should look just as good in 15-foot letters on top of a company headquarters as it does one sixteenth of an inch tall on company stationery."
Steven Gilliatt, American brand specialist

"I've yet to have a client ask me to make them look smaller than they are."
Bill Gardner (1957), American graphic designer

"You know what killed fashion off? Those f...ing logos. They brought it down to the level of advertising, and that's not fashion, that's Letraset."
Alexander McQueen (1969), British fashion designer

Leave it to the last minute

Nothing like a tight deadline to get the creative juices flowing. Many people perform best when working under pressure, designers are no exception…

———

"Never put off until tomorrow what you can do the day after tomorrow."
Mark Twain (1835-1910), American author

"The way to get started is to quit talking and begin doing."
Walt Disney (1901-1966), American director, animator, producer and entrepreneur

"I find that having a real deadline forces a serious degree of focus."
Primo Angeli (1938), American designer

"For me inspiration only comes with pressure. If I go home at six o'clock at night something is wrong. Something is missing. It doesn't have to be two o'clock in the morning anymore like it used to be. But ten or 11 is usual, as it always takes longer than you think."
Erik Spiekermann (1947), German typographer and designer

"[Fashion] is so fast and so intense. It needs so much input, you always have it in your head. There are also the deadlines. But a deadline also forces you to formulate. Without one, it's actually much harder."
Helmut Lang (1956), Austrian fashion designer

"I love limitations when designing a project… I don't love that period when the deadline is looming and there is no idea yet with the pressure slowly mounting."
Stefan Sagmeister (1962), Austrian graphic designer

god god
god god god
god god
god god g god god god god
god god god god god god dog god god
god god god god god god god god god god
god god god god god god god god
god god god god od god god god god god
god god god god od god god god god god
god god god god od god god
god god god god god god god god
god god god god god god god god god god god
god god god god god god god god god
god g
god g
god g
god g
god god god go god god god god g
god god god go god god god god go
god god g god god god god
god god g god god god god
god god g god god god god
god god g god god god god god god
god god g god god god god god god god
god god god god god god god god god god
god god god god god god god god god god
god god god god god
god g goa goa goa
god go god god god
god go god god
god god god
god god go god god god god god god go
god god go god god god god god god go
god go god god god god go
god go god god god god god goa god
god go god god god god god god god
god go god god god god god god god goa
god go god god god god god god
god god go god god god god god god
god god god god god god god god god god god god god god god
god god god god god god god god god god god god god god god

God is in the details

This rule is often attributed to German-born architect Ludwig Mies van der Rohe (1886-1969), but the motto was also a favorite of German art historian and cultural theorist Aby Warburg (1866-1929). Still, the seed was probably planted by Gustave Flaubert (1821-1980), who said: "Le bon Dieu est dans le détail."

_____

"Beware of the person who can't be bothered by details."
William A. Feather (1889-1981),
American author and publisher

"The details are not the details. They make the design."
Charles Eames (1907-1978),
American architect, graphic and
industrial designer

"Discipline is the god of design that governs every aspect of a project, be it two-, three-, or four-dimensional. 'God is in the details,' said Mies van der Rohe. And he was right."
Massimo Vignelli (1931), Italian
designer

THINK OUTSIDE OF THE BOX

In the 1970s and 1980s consultants introduced the so-called nine dots puzzle which challenged clients to connect all nine dots with four, continuous lines and without lifting the pen from the paper. Solving the puzzle required clients to think outside of the box. Who came up with the puzzle remains somewhat of a mystery. It is said to have been used in-house at the Walt Disney company. But at the same time John Adair (1934), the renowned British authority on leadership, claimed to have introduced the concept of 'thinking outside of the box' back in 1969.

"The answers are always inside the problem, not outside."
Marshall McLuhan (1911–1980), Canadian communication theorist

"If you can't solve a problem, it's because you're playing by the rules."
Paul Arden (1940-2008), advertising creative and writer

"Get back in the box. You may find it difficult to remember why you were trying to get out."
Douglas Rushkoff (1961), American writer, lecturer and author

"If you can't find the right answer, look for the right question."
Andrew Smart (1969), British art director

"Open yourself up to other things that can inspire design rather than looking at design constantly. You have to expose yourself to other worlds to keep your mind more active."
Hussein Chalayan (1970), Turkish Cypriot fashion designer

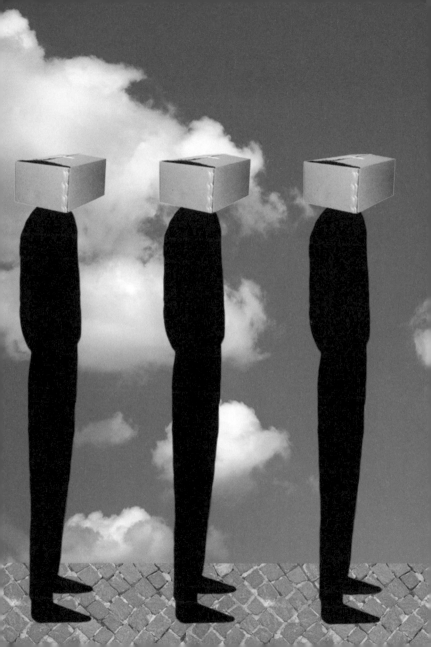

KILL YOUR DARLINGS

"READ OVER YOUR COMPOSITIONS, AND WHEREVER YOU MEET WITH A PASSAGE WHICH YOU THINK IS PARTICULARLY FINE, STRIKE IT OUT."

Samuel Johnson (1709-1784), English author

"In writing, you must kill your darlings," American writer William Faulkner (1897-1962) once said. But he was by no means the first to utter these words. British writer Sir Arthur Quiller-Couch (1863-1944) coined the term 'murder your darlings' back in 1916 in a series of lectures titled *On the Art of Writing*, which were published while Sir Arthur served as Professor of English at Cambridge University: "Whenever you feel an impulse to perpetrate a piece of exceptionally fine writing, obey it – whole-heartedly – and delete it before sending your manuscripts to press. Murder your darlings."

"Remove your favorite bits without crying."
Bo Bergström (1946), Swedish author, lecturer and creative director

"Kill your darlings, kill your darlings, even when it breaks your egocentric little scribbler's heart. Kill your darlings."
Stephen King (1947), American author

"Most of my work consisted of crossing out. Crossing out was the secret of all good writing."
Mark Haddon (1962), British novelist and poet

"Save your darlings, kill the editor."
Campaign by Screenvision

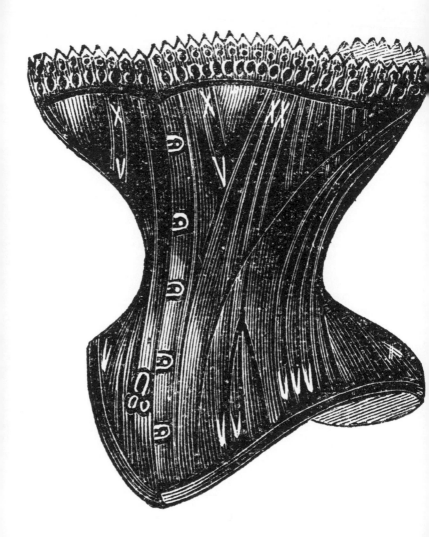

Never sacrifice style for comfort

Oh how we suffer for fashion. Dedicated followers of fashion have always been willing to put up with a fair amount of discomfort in the name of style. But while the days of constricting corsets and suffocating gowns are long gone, the fashion-crazed consumer's apparent willingness to suffer in style remains.

"I buy my shoes a size too small. I like the way it feels."
Karl Lagerfeld (1938), German fashion designer

"I base my fashion taste on what doesn't itch."
Gilda Radner (1946-1989), American actress and comedian

"We've become obsessed with comfort. I actually don't like that. I think you should suffer sometimes to be attractive and beautiful."
Tom Ford (1961), American fashion designer

"I don't think my shoes should be uncomfortable for the sake of fashion. If a woman is uncomfortable, it's reflected in her face and it doesn't leave a nice aperture. But I don't like shoes that look comfortable."
Christian Louboutin (1963), French shoe designer

"The person who uses my products may actually suffer, because ergonomics and functionality are not my aim."
Ron Gilad (1972), Israeli industrial designer

DESIGN IS

rule
38

EVOLUTIONARY:
TURN MISTAKES
AND ACCIDENTS
INTO OPPORTUNITIES

Coca Cola. Cornflakes. Chocolate chip
cookies. The microwave. The post-it.
All were created by accident, rather than
designed by intent. Mistakes turned into
moneymakers. Viva la Evolución!

"OF THE 200 LIGHT BULBS THAT DIDN'T WORK, EVERY FAILURE TOLD ME SOMETHING THAT I WAS ABLE TO INCORPORATE INTO THE NEXT ATTEMPT."

Thomas Edison (1847-1931), American inventor

"The person who doesn't make mistakes is unlikely to make anything."
Paul Arden (1940-2008), advertising creative and writer

"The paradox is that when we model future designs on past successes, we are inviting failure down the line; when we take into account past failures and anticipate potential new ways in which failure can occur, we are more likely to produce successful designs."
Henry Petroski (1942), American professor of civil engineering

"Creativity is allowing yourself to make mistakes. Design is knowing which ones to keep."
Scott Adams (1957), American author and cartoonist

"Keep in mind that most of the projects that you'll design will be refused, this is normal. Keep on trying to find the right manufacturer. If you want to achieve something on a technical level, to reach a particular goal, then be confident and watch out for new materials. Ask the right questions… and speak with the right people."
Inga Sempé (1968), French designer

"The number of projects that we began is much larger than the number that has been brought to completion. Many of them had to be discontinued or rejected; in a demanding and competitive environment, occasional failures are an inevitable part of development work."
Ronan (1971) and Erwan Bouroullec (1976), French designers

The medium is the message

In 1964 a Canadian communication theorist by the name of Marshall McLuhan (1911-1980) published the book *Understanding Media: The Extensions of Man*. In it he coined the phrase 'the medium is the message', which quickly became a popular catchphrase. McLuhan used the sentence again in his 1967 book *The Medium is the Massage: An Inventory of Effects*. The error in the book's title was due to a mistake by the typesetter. Legend has is that upon seeing the typo McLuhan exclaimed: "Leave it alone! It's great, and right on target!"

"In a culture like ours, long accustomed to splitting and dividing all things as a means of control, it is sometimes a bit of a shock to be reminded that, in operational and practical fact, the medium is the message. This is merely to say that the personal and social consequences of any medium – that is, of any extension of ourselves – result from the new scale that is introduced into our affairs by each extension of ourselves, or by any new technology."
Marshall McLuhan (1911–1980), Canadian communication theorist

"Word of mouth is the best medium of all."
William Bernbach (1911-1982), American advertising executive

"The medium is the message. This is an overall rule of thumb for baby boomers. Boomers also tend to confuse emotions for thoughts, sentimentality for sensitivity and public relations for public policy."
Brad Holland (1943), American illustrator

"I saw the political angle for *Obey Giant* as 'the medium is the message'. When something is illegally placed in the public right-of-way the very act itself makes it political. My hope was that in questioning what *Obey Giant* was about, the viewer would then begin to question all the images they were confronted with."
Shepard Fairey (1970), American artist, illustrator and graphic designer

"In graphic design there is usually a defined medium or message, and it's the designer's role to push and challenge the restrictions to create something that communicates."
Daniel Eatock (1975), British designer

The client is always right

Arguably, one of the more controversial rules, implying that he who pays the piper calls the tune.

"I like things that are playful; I like things that are happy; I like things that will make the client smile."
Paul Rand (1914-1996), American graphic designer

"Public recognition is important because it makes every designer more of an equal partner for the client. As long as we are considered a lower form of production service, clients will not involve us properly and will not pay us the money our work deserves."
Erik Spiekermann (1947), German typographer and designer

"Each client is a partnership, a conversation. You're only going to be able to go as far as they wish to go..."
Lindy Roy (1963), South African architect

"The client may be king, but he's not the art director."
Von R. Glitschka (1966), American graphic designer and illustrator

Design is made by the client, designers only push some buttons

Shoes and bags must always match

Is it an actual fashion rule or just a great excuse for women to buy even more handbags and shoes? You decide.

———

"I love looking hooked-up! Just like when I was a little kid, my shoes match my bag that matches my belt – only now it's likely to be matching Gucci or D&G."
Kimora Lee Simmons (1975), American model and creative director Phat Fashions

"Shoes and bags can be made from the same material, but shouldn't be of the same design. Three straps on the shoe and three matching straps on the bag doesn't work."
Jan Jansen (1941), Dutch shoe designer

"Whereas fashion once dictated the rules – like matching handbags and shoes – it now breaks them to move forward."
Carmel Allen, author of The Handbag: To Have and To Hold *(2002)*

Turn it upside down

… and if it still looks great, you're on the right track.

———————

"You can't turn a thing upside down if there's no theory about it being the right way up."
Gilbert Keith Chesterton (1874-1936), British writer

"If you turn things upside down, you quickly realise what works and what doesn't."
Siebe Tettero (1958), Dutch architect and designer of Viktor & Rolf's upside-down store

"Our process is always upside down."
Viktor Horsting (1969), Dutch fashion designer and one half of Viktor & Rolf

"I have my tricks and habits, I suppose. Looking at things upside down is helpful."
Cyrus Highsmith (1973), font designer

"Effective communication contains an element of surprise, and often the best way to solve a problem is to turn it on its head."
Why Not Associates (founded in 1987), British graphic design company

THIS SIDE UP

Trust no-one.
All clients are bastards.
Eat more fish.

The client-designer relationship can be a precarious one. But power struggles, creative conflicts, delays in payment and the odd lawsuit aside, both parties know that at the end of the day they need the other person to make the magic happen. Let's hear it for the codependent relationship.

"There is no such thing as a bad client – there are only bad designers and part of our job is to do good work and get the client to accept it."
Bob Gill (1931), American graphic designer

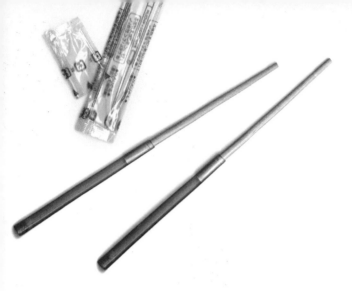

"Every night I pray that clients with taste will get money and clients with money will get taste."
Bill Gardner (1957), American graphic designer

"I have found the best people to work with are gay men. They never have to 'run it past their wives'."
Rodney Davidson (1957), American graphic designer

"As a designer you hope that a client will establish a framework, have its own opinion concerning the field in question and have a vision of the collection it is seeking you build up. Apart from that a client needs to have confidence in me as a designer, to provide me with room and respect at the ideas stage, to provide input during the actual design process and to provide support at the execution stage."
Hella Jongerius (1963), Dutch designer

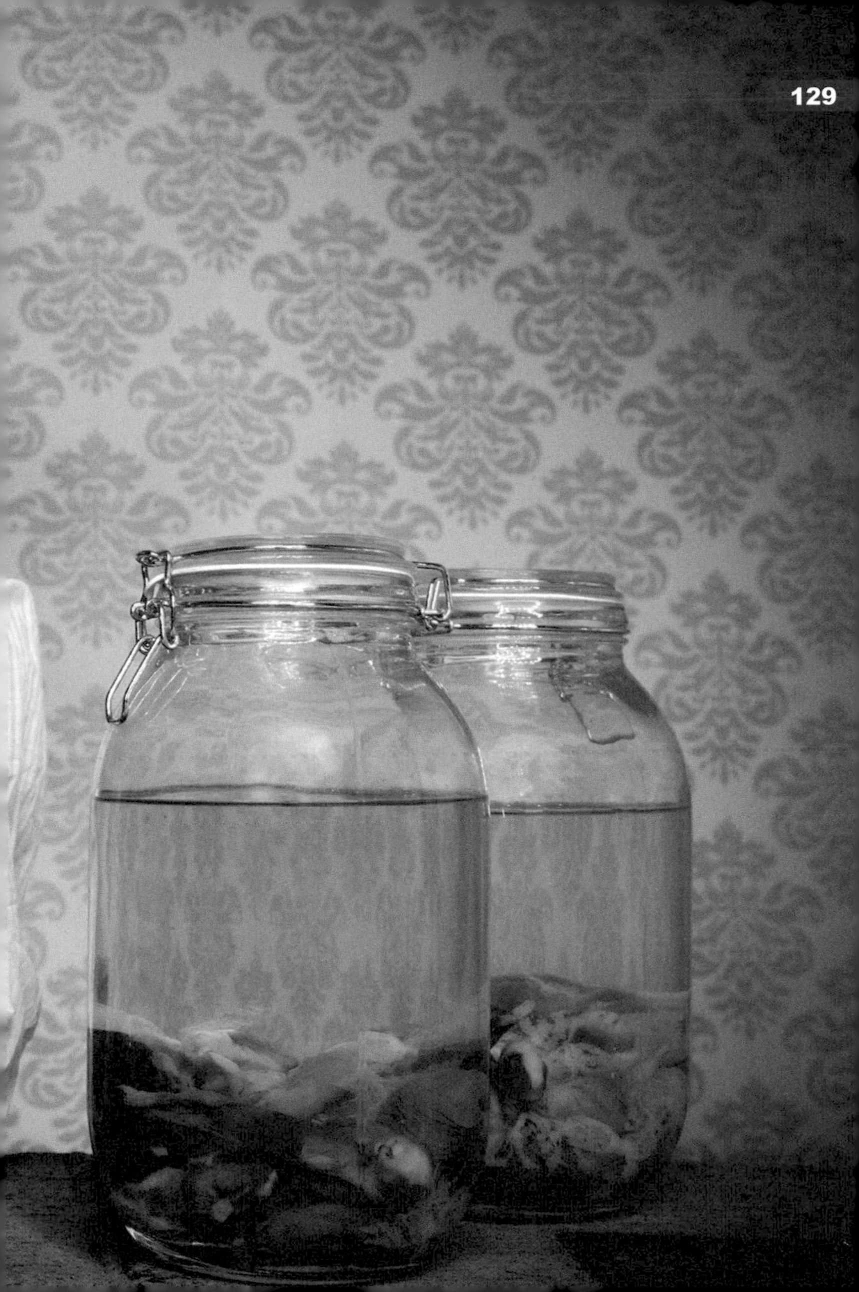

Less is more

Anorexia bracelet

The motto 'less is more' is forever linked to architect Ludwig Mies van der Rohe (1886-1969), but was actually mentioned first in a poem. In the 1855 poem *Andrea del Sarto* by Robert Browning (1812-1889) to be precise.

"Less is not necessarily more. Being a child of Modernism I have heard this mantra all my life. Less is more. One morning upon awakening I realized that it was total nonsense, it is an absurd proposition and also fairly meaningless. But it sounds great because it contains within it a paradox that is resistant to understanding. But it simply does not obtain when you think about the visual history of the world… However, I have an alternative to the proposition that I believe is more appropriate. 'Just enough is more'."
Milton Glaser (1929), American graphic designer and illustrator

"Less is only more where more is no good."
Frank Lloyd Wright (1867-1959), American architect

"Less is a bore."
Robert Venturi (1925), American architect

"Buy less, think more."
Jil Sander (1943), German designer

"Think more, design less."
Ellen Lupton (1963), American graphic designer, writer and curator

"Less IS more. Just look at the invoice."
Stephen Banham (1968), Australian graphic designer

Good design is for life

Design is for life, not just for Christmas. The implication is that while fashion is fleeting, design, or more to the point, *good* design endures.

"As designers, we have two kinds of responsibility, one to our clients and the other to society. We have a responsibility to our client not to design something that will become obsolete quickly; his investment should be justified; he should have something that will last. If a designer feels the responsibility to give the client something that's up-to-the-moment, then when that's obsolete, the client will get something else. This goes back to the notion of obsolescence, fashion, and trends. From my point of view, all are equally detestable. We have a responsibility to society to look for meaning in design, structure, and information, in such a way that will last a long time, not be something you have to throw away."
Massimo Vignelli (1931), Italian designer

"Design should be interested in cultivating the willing of longevity that represents one of our own features and longevity itself is one of the most modern and elegant criteria, opposite to fashion's bulimia."
Philippe Starck (1949), French designer

"I'm always convinced it's essential to return to base, to simple solutions. When you get tired of an object after six months, well that's not true design. True design is the kind that finds ideas that stand the test of time."
Damian Williamson (1974), Stockholm-based designer

design

240ml

KNOW YOUR AUDIENCE

You can't design in a vacuum. Design is used, seen, felt and experienced by people. In order to create good design you'd better know who these people are and what they want.

"To whom does design address itself: to the greatest number, to the specialist of an enlightened matter, to a privileged social class? Design addresses itself to the need."
Charles Eames (1907-1978), American architect, graphic and industrial designer

"The philosophy behind much advertising is based on the old observation that every man is really two men – the man he is and the man he wants to be."
William A. Feather (1889-1981), American author and publisher

"Even if it is true that the average man seems most comfortable with the commonplace and familiar, it is equally true that catering to bad taste, which we so readily attribute to the average reader, merely perpetuates that mediocrity and denies the reader one of the most easily accessible means for aesthetic development and eventual enjoyment."
Paul Rand (1914-1996), American graphic designer

"I'm always my first customer. If I can't imagine having or using a particular object, I won't design it either."
Ingegerd Råman (1943), Swedish product and glassware designer

"A common mistake that people make when trying to design something completely foolproof is to underestimate the ingenuity of complete fools."
Douglas Adams (1952-2001), English author

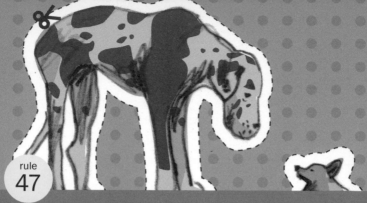

"IF YOUR IMAGE DOES NOT WORK,
PUT A DOG IN IT. IF IT STILL
DOES NOT WORK, PUT A BANDAGE
ON THE DOG."*

PICK YOUR
VERY OWN DOG!

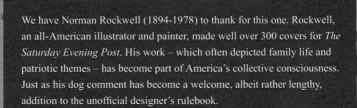

We have Norman Rockwell (1894-1978) to thank for this one. Rockwell, an all-American illustrator and painter, made well over 300 covers for *The Saturday Evening Post*. His work – which often depicted family life and patriotic themes – has become part of America's collective consciousness. Just as his dog comment has become a welcome, albeit rather lengthy, addition to the unofficial designer's rulebook.

*The rule is said to be taken from the following Rockwell quote: "If a picture wasn't going very well, I'd put a puppy in it."

Don't let bad design hurt great content

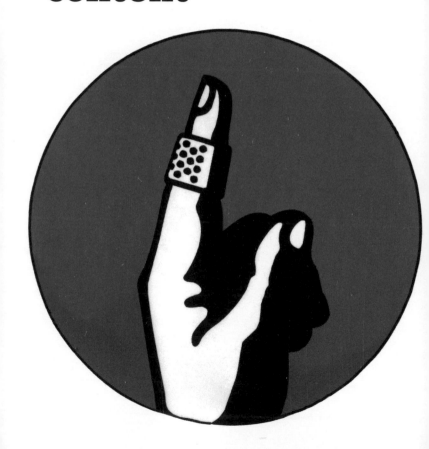

Life's simply too short to drink bad wine, wear uncomfortable shoes or live with bad design.

"Today the emphasis of style over content in much of what is alleged to be graphic design and communication is, at best, puzzling."
Paul Rand (1914-1996), American graphic designer

"Bad design is where the customer thinks it's their fault that something doesn't work. So if you can't make your GPS device work in your car – I mean, there should be a riot because they're so poorly designed! Instead, the user thinks, 'Oh, I'm not very smart, I can't make this GPS thing work.' People should demand more from the things they own, they need to demand that things work."
David Kelley (1951), American designer and engineer

"Content precedes design. Design in the absence of content is not design, it's decoration."
Jeffrey Zeldman (1955), American author on web design

"Content comes first... yet excellent design can catch people's eyes and impress the contents on their memory."
Hideki Nakajima (1961), Japanese graphic designer

"I wish people would be more critical of design, and of designers, who are responsible for designing some pretty nasty stuff."
Marc Newson (1963), Australian designer

"If a design is good you don't ask questions, you simply enjoy."
Richard Hutten (1967), Dutch designer

[Insert buzzword]
is the
new
black

The actual origins of the phrase remain something of a mystery, although Diana Vreeland (1903-1989) usually gets the credits. Back in 1962 the renowned fashion editor was shown an Oriental-looking piece of pink fabric after which she exclaimed: "Pink is the navy blue of India." Black became the new navy blue and the rest is history.

"I'm not that interested in fashion...
When someone says that lime-green is
the new black for this season, you just
want to tell them to get a life."
*Bruce Oldfield (1950), British fashion
designer*

"Innovation is the new black."
*Michael Bierut (1957), American
graphic designer and design critic*

"Design is the new advertising; it is the
new media and the new research."
*Marc Gobé, designer and brand
consultant*

Dress your age

(not your shoe or waist size)

Age-old adage that calls for age-appropriate dressing.

"Clothes that are too young paradoxically make their wearer look older. Remember that the interesting men of the world like women who appear youthful but who are not pathetic carbon copies of the girls they were. On the other hand, clothes that are too sophisticated do not imbue the youthful wearer with the *femme fatale* look she longs to achieve but tend, on the contrary, to give her a comically childlike appearance."
Edna Woolman Chase (1877-1957), former editor-in-chief Vogue

"As you grow older, cover up. Aging flesh is not appealing."
Edna Woolman Chase (1877-1957), former editor-in-chief Vogue

"There is no fashion for the old"
Coco Chanel (1883-1971), French fashion designer

"The correlative of act your age has often been dress your age. Which is only to put in abeyance what, with everlasting fascination, fashion covers up: however you dress – man, woman, man-woman, or… what? – you are inevitably dressed with age."
Herbert Blau (1926), American author, theater director and professor

"A woman is as young as her knees."
Mary Quant (1934), British fashion designer

"I'm looking forward to growing old. Ponytails look good with white hair."
Karl Lagerfeld (1938), German fashion designer

"I see lots of mothers buying high fashion and couture for toddlers – I think it's disgusting. There's Gucci and Burberry for three-year-olds. I just don't believe children should wear designer clothes at this age."
Iman Bowie (1955), Somali supermodel

BREAI
THERL

The mother of all design rules, which is why it is only fitting to end this book with this particular rule.

———————

"Rules are overrated. They need to be changed by every generation. That is your most important mandate: if it's not broken, break it."
Richard Serra (1939), American sculptor and video artist

"I have always believed that breaking rules is what makes clothes interesting. It is what I've done in different ways for my entire career. I love mixing fabrics and shapes in unexpected ways – the classic with the modern, the rugged with the elegant. There are no limits, as long as it's done with a certain taste level."
Ralph Lauren (1939), American fashion designer

"I think fashion is about suspense and surprise and fantasy. It's not about rules."
Wolfgang Joop (1944), German fashion designer

LES

"By all means break the rules, and break them beautifully, deliberately, and well. That is one of the ends for which they exist."
Robert Bringhurst (1946), American poet, typographer and author

"Rules are good. Break them."
Tibor Kalman (1949-1999), Hungarian-born American graphic designer

"Game design up to now has been about making rules."
Hideo Kojima (1963), Japanese video game designer

"I hate rules and formulas. That's so boring. It's the opposite of creativity. Rules are ridiculous things that are meant to be broken."
Philip Treacy (1967), British hat designer

"Rules can be broken – but never ignored."
David Jury, author of About Face: Reviving the Rules of Typography (2002)

"It's those who follow authority blindly who are the real danger."
Banksy, British street artist

CONTRIBUTORS

1 Hans Eijkelboom
(www.photonotebooks.com)

2 Carine Brancowitz
(www.carinebrancowitz.com)

3 Bea Correa
(www.mindwhatyouwear.com)

4 WARECONCEPTS / ZINIDESIGN
(www.zini.pt)

5 Heller Inc.
(www.helleronline.com)

6 HOLLi CONGER
(www.hollicongerdesigns.com)

7 JR
(www.jr-art.net)

8 Tony the Misfit
(www.flickr.com/photos/tonythemisfit)

9 HANDIEDAN
(www.handiedan.com)

10 Magda Rinkema
(www.magdarinkema.nl)

11 Koen Hauser
(www.koenhauser.com)

- Edwin Oudshoorn
(www.edwinoudshoorn.com)

- Henny Bregman-Oudshoorn

12 Zenodot Verlagsgesellschaft mbH
(www.zeno.org)

13 AMagill
(www.flickr.com/photos/amagill)

14 Luis Menezes
(www.who.pt)

15 Sergio Jiménez
(www.subcoolture.com)

16 FARB
(www.farb.nl)

17 João Fernandes
(www.who.pt)
18 Florine Kammerer
(www.florinekammerer.de)
19 Ricardo Cabral
(www.who.pt)
20 Hugo Tornelo
(www.who.pt)
21 Bas de Reuver
(members.home.nl/bas.de.reuver)
22 Seattle Municipal Archives ©
(www.seattle.gov/cityarchives)
23 Sauerkids
(www.sauerkids.com)
24 Deborah van der Schaaf
(www.deborahvdschaaf.nl)
25 Eva Lindeman
(www.evalindeman.com)

26 JoelZimmer ©
(www.flickr.com/photos/joelzimmer)
27 Kevin Lawver ©
(www.flickr.com/photos/kplawver)
28 TINKEBELL.
(www.tinkebell.com)
29 Mirjam Muller
(www.mirjam-muller.com)
- TINKEBELL.
(www.tinkebell.com)

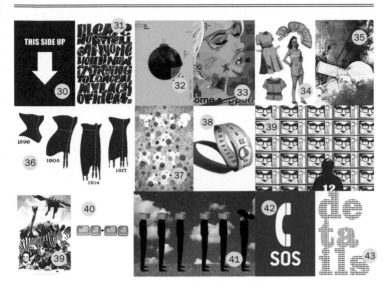

30 Ramelan Sadjid
(www.boomerang.nl/alle-werken/ramelan)
31 Enkeling
(www.enkeling.nl)
32 Cristiana Couceiro
(www.who.pt)
33 DTM_INC
(www.boomerang.nl/alle-werken/dtminc)
34 Ana_ng ©
(www.flickr.com/photos/ana_ng)
35 Sara Franco
(www.who.pt)
36 Haabet
37 Zeptonn
(www.zeptonn.nl)
38 Wondering Boys
(www.wonderingboys.com)

39 Gregori Saavedra
(www.who.pt)
40 Newrafael ©
(www.newrafael.com)
41 Clarisse Earp
(www.clarisseearpillustration.blogspot.com)
42 Visualpanic ©
www.visualpanic.net
43 BORN'84
(www.born84.nl)
WHO- creative talents agency
(www.who.pt)
Unit CMA
(www.unit.nl)

INDEX

INDEX BY NAME

Thanks to:
Dingeman Kuilman (www.premsela.org)
Vanessa van Houtum (www.premsela.org)
Premsela, Dutch Platform for Design and Fashion (www.premsela.org)
Four Weeks of FreeDesigndom (www.freedesigndom.com)
Lemon Scented Tea (www.lemonscentedtea.com)
Annemiek van Grondel
Niki Yocarini (www.unit.nl)
And special thanks to Maria Gasieniec of WHO- creative
talents agency (www.who.pt)

THIS SID